Three Pampered Pugs

The Patriotic Pet Contest

by
Sandra Kitabjian

Illustrated by
Karine Makartichan

Copyright © 2019 by Sandra Kitabjian

All rights reserved. No part of this book may be used or reproduced in any manner whatsoever without the express written permission of the publisher.

ISBN 978-0-578-59816-1

Three Pampered Pugs – The Patriotic Pet Contest
Book and cover design by Sose Bejian
Illustrations by Karine Makartichan

First edition, 2019

Three Pampered Pugs@threepamperedpugs

For
Khloe, Khasi, Kash, Leah and Rocco
~ Love Mimi

With special thanks to
Linda Ammazzaorsi, Sose Bejian, Karen and Paul Sookiasian

"Good Morning," mom said
to her three pampered pugs.

"Today is the Fourth of July!"

"You see that is why wherever you look,
flags are flying high."

"There'll be barbecues
and parades to attend,
Patriotic displays, what a sight!"

"Once the sun goes down,
we'll wait patiently,
for the fireworks in the night."

"But before we go,
there's one more thing,
we must get ready to do."

"I will need to take some photographs
of the three of you."

"The county newspaper is having a contest,
I just read about."

"I'm sure if we enter, you three will win,
that I have no doubt."

"I have t-shirts and hats,
in red, white, and blue
that I bought for this special day."

"So let's get ready as quick as we can,
so we can be on our way."

 Mom dressed the pugs
in their t-shirts and hats,
and sat them side-by-side.

The three of them looked as cute as can be,
flaunting their patriotic pride.

Mom knew the pugs would only sit still,
for just a moment or two,
So she offered them some tasty treats,
to calm the feisty crew.

The photo shoot was over,
it was a job well done.

Now the pugs were ready
to have lots of summertime fun.

Out to the backyard
the three of them hurried,
the festivities were underway.

All were eager to celebrate,
America's birthday.

They ate burgers and hotdogs,
some corn on the cob,
even an ice cream or two.

Now patiently waiting
for the sun to go down,
was the only thing left to do.

Before too long, a dazzling display
of fireworks lit up the night.

It was the perfect end to a fun filled day,
now the pugs would be sure to sleep tight.

The very next morning
Mom said to the three,
" I have a wonderful surprise!"

"I got the results of the contest we entered,
and look, you won first prize!"

In Memory of
Mia, Bella and Rocco,
my *Three Pampered Pugs.*

www.ingramcontent.com/pod-product-compliance
Lightning Source LLC
Chambersburg PA
CBHW061752290426
44108CB00028B/2966